Table of Contents

Introduction 1

Chapter 1: Real Estate Investing for Beginners 3

    How do I get Started with Real Estate? 3

    Busting Some of the Common Myths 6

Chapter 2: Laying the Foundation for Real Estate Success 10

    Understanding the Market Cycle 10

    Assembling your Team 14

    Networking and the Importance of Mentors 16

    LLC, C Corps, and S Corps – which one should I use? 18

    Bringing this All Together 20

Chapter 3: Choosing Your Real Estate Niche 21

    Single-Family Homes 21

    Small Multifamily Unit 22

    Large Multifamily Unit 23

Raw Land 24

Commercial 25

Mobile Home Parks and Mobile Homes 26

Crowdfunding 28

REITs 29

Private Notes 32

Chapter 4: Your Investment Strategy Guide 36

House Flipping 36

Turnkey 37

Live-In House Flips 39

Commercial Rentals 41

Real Estate Development 43

Wholesaling Real Estate 44

Focusing on One Niche 45

Chapter 5: Hunting for the Perfect Real Estate Deal 47

Hitting the Town – Driving Around the Local Area for Deals 48

Eviction Records 49

Online Marketplaces 52

Craigslist 53

REAL ESTATE INVESTING CRASH COURSE

The #1 Step-By-Step Guide for Beginners' Wealth Creation Through Real Estate Wholesaling, Rental Property Investing, Home Buying, & Flipping Houses & Apartments

DEAN WEAVER

Wholesalers 54

Chapter 6: Financing Your Real Estate Empire 57

Cold, Hard cash.. 57

Owner Financing 58

Portfolio Lenders... 59

Conventional Mortgage 62

Hard Money... 63

Private Money.. 64

203K Loans 66

FHA Loans 68

Partnerships 69

Home Equity Loans 70

Retirement Accounts 72

Commercial Loans.. 73

Chapter 7: Planning Your Exit Strategy..................................... 76

Traditional Selling with an Agent 76

Selling for Sale by Owner (FSBO) 78

The 1031 Exchange 81

Selling with Seller Financing 83

Chapter 8: Making It Passive **86**

    Be the Boss 86

    Working Hard vs. Working Smart 89

    Filling Spaces – Always Keeping your
    Real Estate Filled 90

Conclusion **94**

Introduction

Congratulations on purchasing *Real Estate Investing Crash Course* and thank you for doing so.

The following chapters will discuss everything that you need to know in order to get started with investing in the real estate market. There are a lot of benefits when you decide to work in the real estate market, and you get a lot of different choices on which avenue you want to take. This is why, for someone who really wants to see a good return on investment, the real estate market is the perfect place to start.

This guidebook will take some time to look at the different aspects of starting your own real estate business. We will take a look at the different kinds of buildings that you can purchase, the different strategies that are available, how to start up your own team and learn the market cycle, and even how to enter into your first sale to get the strategies going.

From there, we will look at how you find a good deal on the property to ensure that you can make as much money on the deal as possible and then how to find the necessary funding that is critical for purchasing the property that you want.

After we are done taking a look at how to make all of this happen, we will move on to looking at the steps that you need to grow your own real estate empire. You may start out with just one building or a few properties, but if you really want to see how this can all work and how much you will make on the investment, then you need to learn how to grow that empire. We can then learn how to turn the real estate into a passive income and how to plan your exit strategy when you are done with a property or when you are ready to finish with real estate.

There is so much that you can love when it comes to working in the real estate market. Being able to learn as much as possible about this market and how to get started will make a difference in how much success you can see with this endeavor. When you are ready to grow your own real estate empire, make sure to check out this guidebook to help you get started.

There are plenty of books on this subject on the market and thanks again for choosing this one! Every effort was made to ensure it is full of as much useful information as possible. Please enjoy!

CHAPTER 1:

Real Estate Investing for Beginners

Real estate is one of the best options that you can do when it comes to investing. There is a ton of other investments, but with all of the options that come with real estate— from rentals to house flipping to everything in between— you can find something that will help you earn a good return on investment and do something that you enjoy. Let's take a look at some of the things that you need to know in order to start with real state investing for beginners.

How do I get Started with Real Estate?

One of the first questions that you may have when you first get started in real estate is how you are supposed to start. There are a lot of variables that can come into play here, and they are hard to keep track of all the time. But if you know the right steps to help you out, you will find that with some hard work and a bit of risk, you can make the money that you would like.

The first step is deciding that you want to work with real estate investing and then deciding what kind you want to work with.

We will take a look at some of the different types of real estate investing that you can do, including renting, flipping, wholesaling, and more. Knowing what kind of investing you would like to do will make a world of difference when it comes to working in this market.

Once you know how you would like to invest in real estate, it is time to do your research. You have to make sure that you will work with the right kind of market, that you will be in the right neighborhood, and that you will actually be able to earn enough money with the investment whether you are keeping it for an investment or you are choosing to flip it.

You will also need to take a look at your own finances. It is likely that you will need to leverage this a bit with a mortgage on the property or more than one property. If you don't have some down payment ready and a good credit score, this will become even more difficult over time. Having your finances in order will help you get the money that you need for these properties.

There will be a lot of research that you will need to do when it comes to finding the right property. It is not as easy as picking up the first property that comes on the market. That property may end up being too expensive to re-sell it down the line. It may not be a low enough price for you to get a good rental income from it to cover your costs. There could be properties that will need too much work and will take all of your potential profits to fix them up.

You will need to know how much you can charge when it comes to flipping or renting the home and the amount that it will take to fix up that property. Either way, you can make a big difference in whether you will buy one property or not.

You will also need to know a bit more about the area you would like to invest in. You need to look at the neighborhood, the amenities around you, and the prices as well. This can help you figure out if a potential tenant or buyer will even be interested in living there and if you can actually make a profit in that area.

There is a lot of research and work that is needed in order to get started with this kind of investment. But if you are willing to put in the work and the time, you will find that it is one of the best investment choices around for you in terms of return on investment.

Knowing the area around you and taking the time that is needed to really learn the market and find the property that you want will make all of the difference in the world. When you have the finances and are not rushing through the time to get it done, you will find the perfect properties to build up your empire.

Busting Some of the Common Myths

There are many myths that tend to come up when we are talking about starting in real estate. Many people choose to not get into this form of investing because they think that it will cost them too much or that the whole process will be too hard for them to accomplish. When you can dispel some of the myths and can learn the truth of real estate investing, you will want to jump right in and wonder why you didn't give it a try before.

The first myth that we will look at is that the down payment is the only cost that you have to pay up front. If you go into a deal in real estate with this idea, you are in for a big surprise. Don't get some sticker shock when you go to the escrow company and sign on that dotted line. Your down payment won't be the only cost because you have to pay the closing costs, the termite inspection, the home inspection, and anything else you want done on the property.

The good news with this, though, is that most of the closing costs can be negotiated so keep that in mind. If you need to finance the closing costs, it is possible to ask your lender about the options. For example, the FHA loan will add in some of the closing costs to the cost of the loan.

Along with the closing costs, take a look at the different options that are available with this. You do not necessarily have to come up with the full twenty percent. If you can, that will save you a lot of fees and can cut into the mortgage that you will have to pay off. But there are a number of different loans that you can take out that will serve the purpose of financing your property and won't require a full down payment.

Next on the list is checking out the area. Many people will miss out on the good areas because they are just looking for the property that is the cheapest. But the location does matter. You have to consider the kind of tenant you would like to work with and then move on from there. This will help you find the perfect location for the kind of person you would like to rent or sell to.

Another myth that you may deal with is that a single-family home will always be more affordable. The list price of many multifamily dwellings may seem like they come with a higher price tag than some of the single-family homes but consider how much they can make. If you can get a multifamily home that only costs a few hundred dollars extra a month but you can charge rent to eight people rather than one, doesn't it make more sense and become more affordable to go with the second option?

Be careful of the next issue. You should purchase the property without doing a home inspection. This is a dangerous idea. Sure, you can get away without a home inspection, and sometimes you will do just fine not doing one.. But this is an investment, and you are putting a lot of time and money into the whole endeavor. If you are not willing to put in a little money to do a home inspection, then real estate may not be the best choice for you.

It is always a good idea to do a home inspection whether you plan to rent or flip the property. You never know what is hiding in the home that could end up being a big expense and sometimes even the sellers don't know the problem. For example, if the children or someone else is selling a property after the owners passed away, how are they supposed to know what may be wrong with the property without the inspection? Then some sellers may likely be less than honest with you, and you don't want to fall into this either.

A home inspection will probably cost you around $600 to complete, but it is so worth it. If something big comes up, you can renegotiate the price, walk away, or make the seller fix it for you. If you go without the inspection and decide not to do it at all, you are stuck if you find the problem after you own the property.

Working with a real estate agent is a good idea as well. When you are the buyer of the property, you can get all of the expertise and more of an agent—all for free. Having a real estate agent makes it much easier for you to get things started and will ensure that you will get the best deal and can go through and do well with the sale. If you have never bought a home or your personal residence is the only one that you have bought, this is even more important.

Finally, Many different investors will tell you that you can get into the market and get rich overnight without doing any actual work. While you can make a lot of money in real estate, you do have to put in work. You have to learn about the market, figure out how much you can afford and make on the property, how to fix it all up, and more.

If you think that you can get going in a real estate business without having to put in the work, you will be in trouble. True professionals in this business know what it takes, and they know that it takes some time. If you are not willing to put in the work and be a true professional in the real estate market, it is time to give up now because you are more likely to fail in the process.

Working in real estate can be a great investment. There are so many different choices that you can make when you are working in this kind of market and you get the benefit of being able to choose one or more that is the best for you. Knowing how to get started and having a good idea of some of the common myths that will show up in this kind of market and in this kind of investment will make a world of difference in the results that you can get.

CHAPTER 2:

Laying the Foundation for Real Estate Success

Now that we know a bit about investing in the real estate market, it is time to lay down some of the foundations to help you see the results that you want with working in the real estate market. We need to take a look at what the market cycle is all about, how to assemble the team that you need for some good success, the importance of having a mentor and networking on a regular basis, and how to decide what kind of entity you will be for this kind of business. So, let's get started!

Understanding the Market Cycle

The first thing that we need to take a look at is the market cycle. This is important to understand because it will influence when you purchase a property and when you will sell it if that is your goal. If you get in on the right part of the market cycle, you will be amazed at how much you can save and how little you can buy some of these properties.

The first phase of this will be the recovery phase. This is the bottom that the housing market will go. Occupancies are likely at or near their low point with a little bit or even no demand for space. There is also a minimal amount of leasing going on. You won't see any new construction going on when the market is here, and the rental rate growth will either be flat or negative. Sometimes the rent may grow, but it's not keeping up with inflation.

This is the time when the market will be down. Most people are worried about the market and are not purchasing. Those who own homes may have paid too much in a previous cycle, which we will talk about in a bit, and won't be able to afford the mortgage. Short sales and foreclosures are common during this time, and many people resort to renting. Identifying the beginning of this phase will be difficult. Soon, the market will start going up, but it is hard to tell at this point if it will go up or if it will continue to go down.

The neat thing for a real estate investor is that you are able to purchase great properties for a bargain price. Sure, some will need to have some work done, but the price will be worth it. When the market goes back up (You may have to hold onto a flip for a number of years and rent it out in the meantime if the recovery lasts for a long time.), you will either sell for a much higher price or you will be able to increase your rental payments.

After the recovery phase, the expansion phase comes next. During this phase, the market is starting to see a bit of an upturn from before, and buyers are starting to have a bit more trust and faith in how the market is doing. You may see that GDP and the economy are going up during this time as well, and the job growth in that area seems to be strong.

Those who are renting their properties will find that the occupancy rates are better and they are able to charge more for rent. Rentals will start approaching the level that people feel is worth their time to work with new construction, and in certain markets, the surge ahead will go fast. Development will start showing up more during this phase. And at one point, you will see that there is an equilibrium that happens between the supply and demand.

If the market is starting to turn up, this is still a good time for you to purchase a property and jump into the market. There will still be a lot of growth, and the properties that are available will still be at a decent price even if they are not at the prices they were before. This allows you to work at getting a rental or a house flip for a good price and then list it on the market while the prices keep edging up.

The next phase of the market cycle is the hyper-supply. This is when the equilibrium that we talked about before starts to tip over into excess. Oversupply of space can cause some overbuilding that can be a problem and some pullback in demand because of a shift in the economy. You will see that hyper-supply will be marked with some rising vacancies.

Many people get into this stage and aren't paying attention. Lots of building is going on, but it is at a much faster rate than the supply is. While supply may be high for some time, it is likely that it will catch up and not as many people will need those buildings, but the construction will keep on going. This causes prices to still rise even though there aren't any interested buyers.

Investors will still jump in on this part. If you don't have a property by now, then it is time to wait it out. If you purchase in this state, you will end up paying way too much for the property, and you won't be able to sell it for any more than what you paid and most likely for a lot less overall. This is a dangerous time to get into the market because it is a lot of speculation and it is full of people who don't really know how the market works at all.

However, if you want to sell a property that you purchased during one of the first two stages, this is the perfect time to do it. The prices of the homes on the market are high, and you can price yourself competitively and sell. And since you were able to purchase it for such a low price, you get the benefit of making a nice profit.

Finally, we are at the recession. At some point, the hyper-supply stage will result in the supply being too high for the demand. This means that there will be more and more vacancies in the market. Rental growth during this time will start to fall, and they may be negative or fall below the rates of inflation. In addition, owners can hope to get more out of them may start to offer more concessions and rent reductions in the hopes of getting more tenants.

Being able to set yourself up to purchase at the right time and to know when to sell is so critical when it comes to working in this kind of market. If you can set it all up to your advantage, you will buy at the right time and sell at the right time to increase your potential profits. No one knows the exact time of the market cycle. There is no way to tell exactly when there will be a reversal in either direction, but being prepared and recognizing the signs of each will help you see more success.

Assembling your Team

Now that we know a bit more about the market cycle, it is time to take a look at the team that you should consider assembling. If you want to see some good success with this endeavor, you will not be able to do it all alone. You have to assemble a team of people who will be there to support you, to answer your questions, to help you with the legal stuff, and even to help you fix up the properties that you buy.

The first thing you should consider adding to your team is a real estate professional. As a buyer, the agent will be free for you. The seller will pay the commission for the agent even if they are not personally working with the agent when they sell the home. This means that you can get the help and the expertise of the agent— without costing you anything— so it is definitely worth your time.

During this process, the agent can help you look for properties, help you network, give you names for contractors and potential tenants, help with the inspections, help negotiate an offer, and more. They are a wealth of knowledge, and having one to help you out through this process, especially if this is the first property you have purchased, will make a world of difference.

If you do not work with a realtor, make sure that you have a real estate attorney. They can provide you with the various documents that you need when buying and selling property. They can even help you to make the lease that you need on your rental properties. As a beginner, you may not know how to work with some of these legal documents, so working with a real estate attorney can help.

You also want to take a look at some contractors to help you out. Whether you will use the property as a rental or plan to flip the property, to get a good deal, you will probably need to fix it up. It is possible that you can do some of the work yourself. But there may be other work, like plumbing and electrical, that you will want to bring in the professionals. Having a list of a few contractors you trust and are willing to work with on a regular basis will make a world of difference in how quickly you can get them there and how much money you will spend or lose.

Having a good loan officer on your side can help. It is likely that you will not want to stop with the real estate endeavor with just one building, no matter how much you make from it. Having someone, usually at a local bank, who is there and understands what you are doing and can walk you through the process to make it easier over time, will make a big difference in the amount of success you will have when it is time to get another loan.

It takes a lot of people to ensure that your real estate adventure will work the way that you want. Taking your time to assemble this team and thinking of all the things that can happen with the real estate will make the difference in how successful you are in the long run.

Networking and the Importance of Mentors

Networking will be your best friend when it comes to the world of real estate. It will ensure that you can find the tenants or the sellers and buyers that you need to get the work done. The secret to being successful with buying a real estate property is to make sure that you can find one at a good price. If it is listed online or with a realtor, it is more likely to have a lot of competition compared to you hearing through the grapevine about the property and then talking up a deal with them directly. This doesn't mean that you can never go after a sale with an agent, one that is already listed, but you will find that a lot of your best purchases will come from your network.

Once you have the property, you need to focus on ways that you can either rent or sell the property. The sooner you can find either of these, the easier it will be for you to make your money. Having a list of potential tenants and buyers will help you get through the process a bit faster. If you never network and concentrate on finding these kinds of people, it will be hard, and you may spend more time than you would like trying to find someone to take over the property.

During this time, consider finding a good mentor as well. This is someone who has worked in the real estate market for some time and who can spend some time talking with you, answering your questions, and helping you make some smart decisions about the investment all on your own.

Even if the mentor is someone who has worked with rental properties and you want to work with house flipping, they can still provide you with some of the answers that you need when it comes to doing well with real estate. They can help you to find the right property, can point you in the right direction for finding someone to sell or rent it to, and so much more.

LLC, C Corps, and S Corps – which one should I use?

When you get started with your own business, there are a few different options that you can make when it comes to the filing status that you want to give your business. Picking the right one will determine how much control you will have over your business and how much you will be taxed for the business as well.

We will take a moment to list some of the most common options that you can choose when it comes to your business entity. You will then have to choose which one you think will work the best for the kind of endeavor that you want to do. Some of the options that you can choose when it comes to your business entity include the following:

Sole proprietorship

Sole proprietorship will be the default setup if you are the only owner of a business. This one requires little to no paperwork. Many people like this one because they have total control over the business and the taxes that they have go through the personal tax return. The disadvantage of this one is the fact that there isn't any separation between personal and business liability. This can be a bad idea to use if you need to raise some money from other investors to help you get started.

Limited Liability Company or LLC

The next option is the limited liability company or LLC. This one will protect you from any personal liability with the real estate. It will also require a lot less record keeping compared to the other options. The profits and the responsibilities can be divided among the members if there are more than one to work with.

However, if you are working as an LLC, you will find that it is not always the most appropriate if you would like to raise some investor money or venture capital. The entire income for the members of the LLC will be subject to the self-employment tax contributions that will often be higher than what you see with other options.

C Corporation

The next business entity is the C Corporation. This one is nice because it does protect you from any personal liability that may happen as you run your business. It will also be easier for you to raise any of the capital that you need because it is seen by investors and other businesses as an entity that is already established. However, this method will be more expensive to form, and there is an issue of you being taxed two times on the same income. There is also an extensive amount of paperwork that you will need to do with this one.

S Corporation

Finally, you can use what is known as the S Corporation. This one works like the last two and will protect you from personal liability. This one will also have the profits pass through the personal tax return, just like with the sole proprietorship. There are only certain kinds of companies that will be eligible for turning into this kind of entity.

Bringing this All Together

Basically, you will need to take some time to work out all of the particulars that come with running your own business. It takes a lot of time and hard work before you can see the results that you want, but that is part of the fun! If you are willing to think about the business that you are running, the kind of business entity you want to be, and the people you want to have on your team, you will find that you are in a much better position to start this business and see it turn into the success that you want!

CHAPTER 3:

Choosing Your Real Estate Niche

One of the neat things that you will enjoy when you get started with the real estate market is that you get to choose from a wide variety of niches that you will want to explore. This gives you a lot of options and a lot of freedom on what you would like to do with your money overall. Not all real estate investors will do the same things, and that is what makes this investment a fun one. Some of the different real estate niches that you can choose from include the following:

Single-Family Homes

The first option is a single-family home. This is any building that you can rent to a family. Sometimes it may have a few individuals living as roommates instead or a different arrangement. But it will include any property that you could imagine a family owning for themselves.

There are a number of benefits of working with this option. First off, if you can find a property in a good neighborhood—one that has good schools, local attractions, and pleasant to be in—it will not be hard to find the tenants that you want or to sell the property to another family. If you are renting, you may find that these tenants are willing to stay for a number of years rather than picking up and leaving right away. This can provide you with a nice steady stream of income for a while.

There are some negatives. First, you can only receive one income from each property. While this income can be more per unit than some of the other options, it still limits what you can do in terms of growth. Plus, if a tenant leaves, you will be without any income until you can get another renter.

Small Multifamily Unit

The next method is a small multifamily unit. This could be something like a townhome or a four-plex. You have more than one tenant, but it is not so large that you have to keep up with hundreds of different tenants and units at the same time. These can often be found in good neighborhoods as well. You can attract the same kinds of tenants as you can with a single-family home, but you get the benefit of receiving rent from four units at once even though the price of the property is not much more than a single-family home.

If you choose to go with this option, there are lots of benefits. You can charge a pretty decent rent because these properties are usually favorable, and you get to charge it on two or more units at a time. The cost of purchasing these is a bit higher, but since you can collect good rent from more than one unit at a time, you can see a big increase in your profits compared to working with a single-family home. Make sure that you screen the tenants well and that you pick a good multifamily unit.

There are a few issues, though. If you cannot charge enough for the rent, you will not recover the losses, especially if one of your tenants leaves and no longer lives in the area. These buildings are often bigger, which means more work and maintenance on your part so you need to think these through ahead of time.

Large Multifamily Unit

You can also choose a large multifamily option if you would like. These will often be apartment buildings, and they can range from twenty to thirty units or even up to hundreds. This means that even with a reasonable rental rate, you can potentially earn a profit from hundreds of people at the same time. These cost a bit more to start with, but if you can maintain them and keep tenants without a high turnover rate, you can make a huge amount of profit in the process.

You will also find that this kind of property has many benefits. You may be able to live in the property and have your own living expenses covered if the building is big enough. Plus, if all of the units are full and have tenants paying their rent on time each month, you can make thousands of dollars a month.

However, there are reasons that not everyone wants an apartment building for this investment. First, there is a lot of work that comes with this kind of property. With all of those units, it means that you need to keep up with all of them and the tenants. These apartments often run into issues because they have a high turnover rate, meaning that you will need to spend a lot of time working to find tenants to fill the building.

Raw Land

Another option is raw land. This one is really helpful if you can keep up with what is happening in your town and you can get a jump ahead of time, purchasing the land before it goes up in value. Then you can sell the land later and earn a big profit.

For example, maybe you see that the town is growing in one direction and it is forecasted that it will keep going with new families and individuals moving into that area. Or maybe there is a new big business that is going up in that area and will make the town grow as well. Your goal would be to purchase this land ahead of time before others catch on. You can get the land for almost nothing, and then when that situation happens, and people want to build and move to that area, you can sell it for a lot of money.

Before all of that stuff happens and the area starts to grow, the land is not going to be worth as much as it will later. Maybe you can get ten acres of land for $100,000. Then you sell off parcels of it to those who would like to have some land to build a new home as the area grows. Maybe you keep the plots large and offer them as an acre each for $50,000. This could give you a total of $500,000 for your effort. Or even half an acre is a big amount for in town, and if you sell for maybe $30,000, you can earn $600,000.

The problem with this is that you need to be accurate with your predictions. You need to do it early enough that you can get the property for a discount before others jump on and the price goes up, and you may have to hold onto it for a bit of time. If you end up being wrong about the growth or the future value over the land, then you will have land that you are not able to sell for as much as you would like.

Commercial

You can also choose commercial properties. This will bring in a new challenge that you will see when compared to working with some of the other options that we have talked about. But there are a lot of different options that you can work with when it comes to this option. You can rent big warehouses, office buildings, strip malls, and more.

Commercial buildings are nice because the tenants that you work with are often going to stay around for a longer time period. They want to make it easy for their customers to find them. If you can provide them with a competitive rate and take care of the building and the grounds and your building is in the right location, then you will find that it is easy to keep your tenants around and make a good income in the process.

There are a few issues that come with this kind of investment, though. First, you have to worry about finding tenants. Whether it is the first tenant or you need to find a new tenant after a previous one leaves, it is sometimes hard in order to find someone who want the space. These are very specialized niches, which makes them harder to find tenants.

Mobile Home Parks and Mobile Homes

Another option is mobile home parks and mobile homes to help you make an income. Some investors will do a combination of the two to help them make their income, but you can choose to do one or the other if you would like.

First, let's look at a mobile home park. This is where you own the land and upkeep it as you can. Then people can purchase mobile homes that are on the land. The tenants will own the property and will pay a bank for the building. But since the building is parked on your land, they will pay you an agreed upon amount to be there on the land. Since the buildings will not move, this is a steady source of income. If someone new moves into the property, then they will start paying the amount on the lease.

Since you can purchase a piece of land for very little but can charge a few hundred a month or more for the land for the homes, this can add up to a lot of money in your pocket. You just need to make sure that you maintain the area and make it somewhere that others will want to live and pick out a good location as well.

Another option is to rent mobile homes. These homes may not be as high quality as the ones you will find with single-family homes. But they will have individual homes where they can live and make their own. You can provide these, maintain them like any other property, and charge rent for it. If you have a bunch of mobile homes in a mobile home park, you may be able to make money on the land and on the mobile home at the same time.

You have to be careful with this, though. Many landlords end up not taking good care of the areas where these parks are, and this will make it hard to get tenants and pay any of your debts. If you are making your own or purchasing an already-made mobile home park, consider how well you can maintain it over the long term so that you can actually earn an income and find the right tenants.

Crowdfunding

If you don't want to put in the actual work that comes with real estate because you don't have time or aren't sure how to make it happen, then doing crowdfunding may be the right option for you. This method allows you to put up the money that you want for real estate, but then you will let another investor do the work.

It is hard to get a traditional loan for one of these real estate properties. Some mortgage lenders will do it, but others will not. This means that the investor may turn to other sources to get the money that they need to make the purchase and earn money, and crowdfunding is one of the options that they will use.

With crowdfunding, you and other people, who have the money but don't want to own the building or do the renovation work, will pool together some money. Then potential investors who want to get into real estate, such as one of the options above, will come and apply for a loan of this money. There are a variety of terms that you can set up, including the interest rate, the amount of time they get to pay it off, and more.

You will earn money on the interest that they pay for the loan, such as what they would do with a traditional mortgage. You are like the bank in this situation, and the investor will be responsible for any of the closing costs as well. If things go well, you will earn a profit from the interest that the investor pays to you as they get the business up and running. If things go wrong, which they shouldn't because you properly vetted this investor ahead of time, you will have a lien on the property and will get to sell that to get the money back.

REITs

The next option is the real estate investment trust or REIT. This is a provision in the tax law that allows individual investors to purchase shares in commercial real estate portfolios that receive income from more than one property. The properties that are found in this kind of portfolio could include places like hotels, healthcare facilities, data centers, apartment complexes, self-storage units, warehouses, retail centers, and office buildings to name a few.

Most of these REITs will specialize in a specific sector of real estate marketing. This helps them to focus their time, energy, and funding on one segment of the real estate horizon. However, these REITs will hold onto different types of properties to their portfolio to help the investors get the most out of their investment as possible.

This brings up the question of how these work. Most of the REITs that you can invest in will have a model that is easy to work with. The REIT leases space, collects the rent on the properties, and then distributes the income as dividends to shareholders. To help make sure that it qualifies as a REIT, a company needs to comply with a few provisions according to the Internal Revenue Code.

To meet this kind of code, there are a few different requirements that must be met. These include owning own a piece of real estate that will generate income for the long term and distribute some of that income to the shareholders. These are the basics of it. You will also need to work with the following rules to fit into this kind of investment:

1. Invest a minimum of 75 percent of all your assets into the U.S. Treasury, cash or real estate.

2. Receive at least 75 percent of your gross income from real property rentals, from interest on mortgages that finance a real property, or from sales when you sell one of your real estate properties.

3. Return a minimum of 90 percent of its taxable income in the form of dividends for the shareholders each year.

4. Have at least 100 shareholders after the first year of being in existence.

5. Have no more than 50 percent of its shares held by five or fewer individuals during the last half of the taxable year.

Sometimes there will be other requirements that need to be present, including the REIT being an entity that can be taxable as a type of corporation in the eyes of the IRS. The enterprise needs to have the management of a board of trustees or directors as well.

There are a few different benefits that come with choosing to invest your money in one of these choices. On the positive, REITs will be easy for you to purchase and sell since they are mostly going to trade on the public exchange. This marketable feature will mitigate a bit of the traditional things that will keep you away from real estate.

For example, when you traditionally work with real estate, it has been known as illiquid. This means that it does take some time to sell or purchase the investment and it is not going to have as much transparency as you would like because it is hard to find reliable information on things like zoning, ownership, and taxes. But the REIT will have SEC regulation, and they need to file audited financial reports so you are able to get all of that transparency that you are looking for.

When it comes to the performance that you see with these, the REITs will offer you some attractive returns and a good amount of stable cash flow along the way. And just having some real estate in your portfolio will add in the diversity that you are looking for and can be a good counterweight to bonds and equities as well.

These are a few downsides to working with this kind of investment, though. First, these will not offer you much when it comes to capital appreciation. As part of their structure, they need to pay 90 percent of the income to their investors. This means that only 10 percent of the income that is tabled can be reinvested back into the enterprise to purchase new holdings.

The dividends that are received from these holdings will be taxed just like regular income. One of the biggest risks that come with these investments is that they will change a lot based on the fluctuations of the real estate market. Plus, like with other investments that you may choose to do, they will not guarantee a profit or protect you from the losses that can come with them. You may find that some of these will come with high transaction and management fees.

Private Notes

The final option that we will take a look at is the idea of real estate notes. These will provide a good investor with a secure amount of returns without having to deal with the risks and the hassles of buying and flipping a fixer-upper, locating tenants, and dealing with all of that.

When most people think about these mortgage notes, they think about some of the giants in the industry, like Wells Fargo and Bank of America. However, it is possible to work with a private note, where an individual investor can do the investing and earn a good return on the investment.

A common type of note will be known as seller financing. This is when the seller enters into an agreement with the buyer, saying that the seller will lend the buyer all or a portion of the purchase price of the home. Often the interest and the principal payments will be structured for a 30-year period just like we see in a traditional loan, but it will require what is known as a balloon payment. This means that the borrower needs to remit the entirety of the leftover principal after five years.

The expectation is that the borrower, during that five-year period, will refinance this into a conventional loan from a regular lender. If the borrower gets to the end of the five years and they are not able to pay the full amount, then the noteholder can foreclose on the property and take it back. The main risk to the investor in the note is that the net sales proceeds of the foreclosure sale may not end up being enough to cover the balance of the note.

These kinds of loans will be used by a borrower who, for one reason or another, cannot qualify for a conventional institutional loan. Sometimes this is not a reflection on their own creditworthiness. For example, under some of the guidelines that are in place, many self-employed borrowers with good credit scores and high income would still not be able to get a conventional loan. Retirees may run into the same problem.

For these reasons, the private mortgage loan can help them get the home that they need. But they will carry an interest rate that is a bit higher. This is what makes them such an attractive thing for the seller. You will also find that these kinds of notes will be easy to sell if you find a robust market at that time. Although their higher than market interest rates can make them more attractive as a buy and hold investment, it is possible that these notes can be sold and later converted into cash if needed.

The concept here of the time value of money will also help control how much someone is willing to pay for this kind of note. With this concept, we are looking at how receiving a dollar today will be worth more than getting that same dollar in the future. There are tools available online that will help you calculate the present value of your future stream of income. What this means is that someone who is selling a private mortgage note can't expect to sell the note for the outstanding principal of that note. Rather, they will only sell it at the discounted present value of the sum of all future payments.

As this chapter has shown, you can do many different things to make some good money in the real estate market. Many people worry that this market will be too hard to get into or are stuck working with one type with no other options. But there are options for real estate investing, some of which require you to get your hands dirty to see a return on investment and others that just need some of your capital. You can choose from any of these to help you determine how you would like to earn the money you need from real estate investing.

CHAPTER 4:

Your Investment Strategy Guide

The next thing that we need to focus on here is the idea of coming up with a good investment strategy to go with your real estate endeavor. There are a number of different methods that you can use that will give you some flexibility and will ensure that you will see the results that you want. Some of the different strategies that you can use include:

House Flipping

House flipping is a great investment strategy that you can use to get started in the real estate market. It does take some time and dedication to make it happen. But if you are ready to work with this kind of investment and you are not scared to do some research and take a bit of a risk, you can see some tremendous results in the process.

House flipping is a great way for you to earn a lot of income at once. The idea is that you find a property that is below market value for one reason or another, purchase it, make some inexpensive fixes to the property, and then list it on the market as quickly as possible. The faster that you can sell the property, the more money you will make. If you hold onto the property for too long, the amount that you pay in taxes, insurance, and mortgage, will eat into your profits pretty quickly.

The idea of house flipping will seem pretty easy, but many different things can come up that will make this a bit harder to do. You have to find a good property that will get you a good return on investment but won't take so much money and time to fix up that it isn't worth your time. You have to get the seller to agree to a lower price that you can afford. And you have to get the work done quickly and find a good buyer so that you don't end up paying the mortgage for several months.

If you can do all of this and sell the property quickly for a good profit, you could do this a few times a year and end up making a very good income. But you have to be organized, have a plan, be ready to put in the work, and be fast to make that into a reality.

Turnkey

The second type of investment strategy is a turnkey property. This will be a fully renovated apartment building or home that the investor can purchase and then rent right away. These properties are purchased from a company that specializes in the restoration of some of the older properties in your area. These firms can sometimes offer services of property management to you, which can minimize the amount of time and effort that can put into the rental.

These properties started to grow a lot in popularity after the decline in the housing market from 2007 to 2008 because it was cheaper to purchase a new home than it was to rent one in most parts of the country. This is a good approach to investing that is appealing to those who would like to gain a bit of exposure to the real estate market, but they don't have the ability or the time to handle renovating a new property or to manage it on their own.

So, you can imagine that these will often be a bit more expensive to work with compared to purchasing and fixing up your own property and renting it. How can you take this kind of property and turn it into a way to make some income at the same time?

When you purchase one of these properties, the expectation is that a new buyer will turn it around and make it available to rent to some tenants. By getting this kind of rental property without the work, the idea is that you can generate revenue through renting the property as fast as possible. The shorter the turnaround, the faster that you can see a good return on your investment.

The effectiveness of one of these properties will be questioned if the goal of this property is to sell it right away rather than rent it. The expenses that may be put towards some of the repairs may help to sell it for more, but there are times when this will not work in your favor.

Before you decide to purchase one of these properties, you need to carefully do your research. Sure, it will be nice to purchase a property that is immediately ready for you to turn around and rent it to others, but you have to figure out if the price is worth it. The company you are purchasing from has to make some kind of income in the process, and if they don't, then why would they sell it? You have to really look and see if the potential profit that you can make will be enough to cover the higher expenses of going for the fully furnished and ready to use kind of property that you will need to do all of the work on your own.

Live-In House Flips

House flips can be a great investment strategy if you know what you are doing. You can pick out a good property that has a lot of potential and will be easy and inexpensive to fix up along the way. You also need to make sure that you can sell the property as well. This can add on a lot of risks, and since it is possible that you can hold onto the property for some time even when it is under contract to be sold, you may lose some money in the process.

One idea that you may want to give a try when you are working with house flipping is the idea of living in the property while you are flipping it. This allows you to save on the other housing expenses that you would normally have and to cut down on the rent or mortgage along with electricity, insurance, and taxes.

You have to make sure that you stay on task with this, though. Sure, this is your temporary home for a bit. But if you are not able to pay attention and stay on the task that you are doing, it is easy to get distracted and not know when it is time to work and when it is time to relax. If you think that you can just come home and not put any work into the project, it is probably best if you keep your work arrangements and your living arrangements separate.

Vacation rentals

Another option that you may want to consider is vacation rentals. These are rentals that those who go on vacations will stay at. Not everyone wants to be stuck in a hotel all of the time. Having the ability to stay in a nice condo or in a house during that time can be more relaxing and fun. And since it allows them to play, relax, and even cook their own meals to save money, they are often willing to pay a little bit more for it.

While you may only be limited to charging $1000 to $1500 a month for a property if someone lives in it full-time, you may be able to charge that and more for someone spending just one week in the property. Since they are on vacation, they get room to spread out and be comfortable. They don't have to stay in a hotel, so people will spend more. Your job is to make sure that you keep the building full by either finding someone or cleaning it yourself after each tenant leaves.

If you decide to do this option, you need to make sure that you pick out good locations. No one wants to go on vacation and end up in a place where they feel unsafe. Even if you do not live in the area, consider making a trip there and checking out the property and the area before you make the purchase. This ensures that people get the best possible visit when they choose you and that you won't have to worry about the safety of your visitors either.

The biggest issue with this investment is finding a property that won't cost you an arm and a leg, that won't need a lot of money to fix up, and that people will want to stay in. Many people want to make sure that they can invest in this, which means the property values are high, and finding a hidden gem can be hard. Once you find it, you need to make sure that the rental price is attractive enough that you can earn a steady income on a regular basis rather than having a lot of time when no one is staying on the property.

Commercial Rentals

Commercial rentals are a great option if you want to try something a bit different. You can earn a good amount of income each month if you can find a good property to purchase and your tenants are likely to stick around for a long time. There are a few downsides that come with this. Commercial rentals are a great place to work with if you aren't interested in having to take care of the tenants all the time, but you would still like a nice steady income from one month to another.

There are a few different types of commercial rentals that you can do. Your choice will depend on where you are, what is available, and what the needs are of the businesses around you. Choosing the right one can make a difference in how much money you can make and the kind of tenants that you are willing to work with.

The first type that you can work with are the warehouses or the buildings for bigger businesses. These are the bigger stores that want a lot of space, such as grocery stores and retail stores. These places want some good real estate that their customers can get to pretty easily. If they are given a good rental price from one year to the next, they are not likely to leave, and you could have a steady tenant for ten years or more if all goes well.

Then there are office buildings. These are a bit smaller, and the way that you rent them will depend on what the building can offer. You could have one big office building that is for one company, such as a doctor's office or a chiropractor. There are also those office buildings that are easy to split up, and you can rent to a few different companies at once. This allows you to earn a good income from more than one place at a time as well.

Strip malls are a great example of working with this. If you plan this out right, you can have five to 10 businesses, sometimes more, all paying rent on one building and then add in space for a few fast food restaurants and more. This means that you can have quite a few tenants paying rent each month, and since these strip malls are often in prime locations, you can make a lot of money on a steady tenant as well.

Real Estate Development

Another option that you can choose when it comes to the real estate business is to work in real estate development. A real estate development is the engine that will propel the growth in this industry. They will figure out which properties need some work and then will grow these and improve this kind of building.

Developers are the ones who help form new areas of town and get businesses, personal property, and more set up and ready to enhance the town. In areas where there are a lot of people moving in, this can be a lucrative position. Pick the right areas and locations where people would like to spend their time and money to live, and you can earn a lot of good money.

Wholesaling Real Estate

The next option is wholesaling real estate. This occurs when one party, who is known as the wholesaler, enters into a contract with the seller of a home. While they are working on that contract, they will market the home to other potential buyers and will assign the contract to one of them. The wholesaler will make a profit on moving that contract over, and it will be the difference between the contracted price they have with the seller and the amount that the buyer pays. The goal in this is to get the home sold before the original contract with the home seller closes so that the wholesaler doesn't actually ever own the home.

The key to this is to add in a contingency to the purchase contract that will ensure that the wholesaler can back out of the deal at any time if they cannot find a good buyer before they close on the home. This will limit some of your risks. You have to be careful, though. It can limit your risk a bit, but many sellers will not be happy about taking on this risk so you may not get them to do it.

It is similar to flipping homes except that the time frame to find the buyer will be shorter, and the wholesaler will not do any repairs on it. Since the wholesaler never purchased the home, it is less risky than flipping. Real estate wholesaling will also involve a lot less when it comes to upfront capital compared to flipping.

For most of these contracts, coming up with the proper amount of earnest money payments will be enough.

If you decide to go with this kind of option, you need to know the market, and your networking skills need to be high. If the wholesaler cannot find a buyer in time, the whole deal can fall through. Depending on the kind of contract that they signed with the original seller, they may end up owning the home for some time and paying the expenses for it. There is some risk with this, but if you can get it all set up the way that you would like, it will be easier for you to get it going without having to own a property or put much money down in the first place.

Focusing on One Niche

One thing that you need to focus on is sticking with one niche. We have spent some time talking about all the different types of real estate that you can work with and you may be excited to get started. But if you cannot keep your focus on one thing at a time, it can be really difficult to get things done.

It is best if you start investing in one category at a time. This may seem hard to limit yourself to one thing when there are so many great options to consider. But it will help you to focus a bit more and will make the process easier. If you take on more than one niche at a time, especially early in the game, you will take on too much, get confused, and end up failing.

After you have gotten the one niche up and running, you can add on more if you like. But make sure that you have a really good grasp on the ideas with that niche and that it is pretty much up and running all on its own with very little help from you. In the beginning, though, it is best if you can focus on the one niche that makes the most sense to you and has caught your attention the most.

There are many different investment strategies that you can work with when you want to enter the real estate market. As you do your research, you may notice that all of them will provide you with a good return on investment and can give you a unique challenge. With that said, find the one that works the best for you and move on from there.

CHAPTER 5:

Hunting for the Perfect Real Estate Deal

The next thing that we need to look at is that you can find some of the best deals. If you end up paying too much for the property or having to pay too much for the property fixes, or a combination of both, you will never be able to make any money on it. This doesn't matter whether you work with rental properties, flipping, or some other method along the way.

This chapter will help you find some of the best deals that you can work with to earn as much profit as you can. This will take some time, and you will not necessarily find the property right away. But with some patience, a lot of research, networking, and looking around, you will find the good deals that you need to start your real estate empire. Some of the places where you should hunt to find the perfect real estate deal include the following:

Hitting the Town – Driving Around the Local Area for Deals

One of the best things that you can do is to hit the pavement and work on finding the properties around town. Driving around and looking to see if there are any for sale by owner, any homes that look like they could use a little bit of love and attention from you, or anything else that will help you find homes that are available for a good deal.

If you find a home that isn't listed but looks like it may need a bit of work, you still have a chance. You can find out who lives there or who owns it. If someone owns it but doesn't live in the property, you may want to contact them, see if they are interested in selling the property, and give them an offer. If someone lives there, talking about your interest in the property may open up the negotiations that you would like.

Networking is an important thing to work with on this as well. You can talk to people you know and even some real estate agents, can to find out when there are some new properties coming up on the market and if any of them will be a good deal.

The best case scenario is that you can find out about a good deal on a property before it gets to the market. This can be great because you can put in a good offer on the property and not have a lot of competition from other home buyers or investors along the way.

The point here is that you need to get out and know the location where you would like to invest. These properties will not fall into your lap. If they end up with a realtor or online, they will either go fast, or they will need a ton of work. That is why no one will want them. Taking the time to learn more about the market, and making some good connections will ensure that you can find the best deals.

Eviction Records

Another place to look is the notices about evictions or the future and potential foreclosures that are on the market. These will not always be listed on some of the traditional channels, which means that you may need to do some legwork to find them. But it is a great way to find a good deal without a lot of competition if it is not publicly listed.

The point behind looking at the eviction listings is that you can target the landlord who is evicting tenants for not paying the rent. This is a good time to catch one of these landlords because they are already feeling pretty frustrated with the property, especially if these evictions are happening on a regular basis. This may be a prime time for them to sell the property. This is also the time when it is most likely the landlord will not have much, if any, cash flow from the property and could be dealing with some financial issues as well.

At this point, it may cross your mind that you don't really want to purchase a property that has trouble with tenants. However, you will not actually purchase the property until the tenant causing all of the trouble is gone. Then you can do the needed repairs and find a better tenant. You may be able to get a better rental price out of the process as well.

To help you start researching some of the listings for evictions, you need to take a look at the legal section in the newspaper first. In most counties, you can find one of these cases as a civil suit. The only problem will be that these cases will also encompass some other cases, such as disputes and lawsuits, and it is hard to figure out the kind of case that is listed.

You will need to identify which cases have been filed by one private party against a second private party along the way. You can take the list of these cases to the courthouse and do some more research to figure out which cases will be evictions.

You want to make sure to avoid certain types of evictions, though. You do not want to work with eviction cases when the filing party will be with an apartment complex or a property management company. To get the best results, your goal is to look for private landlords that can evict a tenant on a smaller property.

You can find a few of these cases in the newspaper, and then you can look them up in the courthouse. If you want to save time, you can skip the newspaper and go to the courthouse. Once you are there, you want to head to the area where these civil cases are filed. The index of these civil cases will often be in a large book that is updated, or it is on a computer in some places. In either of these cases, the counties will list the case's files according to the plaintiff's name and the defendant's name. You can then look for the times when both of these will be private parties.

Something else that you can do is pull up some of the most recent cases. This will ensure that you are working with landlords who are dealing with the eviction right now or in the last few weeks but not ones who had the eviction ten years ago.

As you are going through and finding this information, you want to make sure that you figure out the property address where the eviction occurred. This gives you a good idea of how big the property is and if it is a good choice for you to talk to and gather information about the landlord. You want to at least have their name and address so that you can contact them. Sometimes you can get their phone number, too.

When you decide to proceed, it is important that you make contact in the proper manner. You can do a few things to help you out with this. You want to make sure that you at least send them a regular mail letter as well as an email if you feel that it will work. Let them know who you are and what you are interested in and give them a way to contact you. If they are interested, they will get in touch with you. You do not need to bother or hound them. If they are truly interested in listing the property and getting it off their hands, they will get in contact with you.

Online Marketplaces

There are many different options that you can choose when it is time to look online for a property. You can talk to a realtor about the ones that are the best for your area, but doing a good search of all the different choices around you can ensure that you don't end up missing some of the properties that you want to work with. The more research that you can do, the more that you can find and the more likely that you will choose a property that is just right for your needs.

As you do your research, you are likely to find that there are a ton of different online options that will show you which properties are available. For example, you can look at options like realtor.com, Zillow.com, and trulia.com. Look through all of these and make sure that you are getting the most information for your needs to get the results that you want to find the perfect properties.

Craigslist

You can consider working with Craigslist. There are a lot of properties that are for sale by owner that are listed. Craigslist will offer you a chance to list these properties for free, which makes them an attractive option for those who are trying to reach a big audience and who want to get their home sold. Sometimes, if you are willing to look around a bit, you can find some amazing deals in the process.

Take some time to look around in the area where you would like to invest and see what comes up. If there are some that look like they are a good price, then it is time to do some more research. Just because they are found on this site doesn't mean that you can just pick one and call it good. You are still investing your own money, and you need to pick out a property that will make you some good money.

When you are looking on Craigslist, make sure that you take some time to ask for more pictures, talk to the seller, and learn everything that you can about the property. If it is available, you can go to the local county assessor's office and learn about the taxes and the seller's information. After doing some market research, if you feel that this is still a good property for you to invest in, contact the seller and do a showing. Put in the same amount of due diligence on this property as you would with any other one.

Be careful with this one, though. While it is possible to find a lot of amazing properties that you will want to work with, you do need to show some caution. Craigslist will not do any verifications about the information so it is possible that some ads are fake and you need to be careful about them.

If the seller won't let you see the house, doesn't give you the address, or wants you to send money to them without the benefit of an escrow account for some reason, end the conversation right then and there. You do not need to risk your profits and any of your reputation by falling for something like this. Even if everything looks right on paper but something makes you feel wrong or off about the process, then it is better to walk away and miss out on something good. It saves you from something that could be potentially bad.

Wholesalers

Another place that you can look is a wholesaler. This is someone who has already entered into a contract with a potential seller and who is working on closing the deal. Since the wholesaler doesn't want to own the property for themselves, they are always looking for a potential buyer who would take over the contract in the process.

These wholesalers are often able to get really good prices on the properties that they decide to sign on. While you will pay some fee on the property in addition to the actual amount that it is worth, this is how the wholesaler gets paid. It is still a lot less than a lot of the other properties that you want to work with and can save you a lot of time looking for your own property without any help.

The first thing here though is to do a few calculations. You want to make sure that you can find a property that will be cheap enough that you can make an income after you purchase it. If this doesn't make sense with the numbers that you are looking at, walk away. The wholesaler may be able to find buyers that are investors and buyers who want to just purchase a family home. This means that sometimes you will have a property that works for you and sometimes not. But it never hurts to look.

There are a lot of places where you can look to find the best real estate deals for your own needs. It is important to open up all of the avenues that you can find. You never know when there is a property that may be hidden a little bit and one that may give you a good deal in the process. You just have to have some patience, be ready to do some research, and not jump too quickly on a property until you can look it over, crunch some numbers, and make sure that it is the right one for you.

CHAPTER 6:

Financing Your Real Estate Empire

The next thing that we need to look at is how you can finance your real estate empire. You have to make sure that you will have enough money to purchase any of the properties that you would like to use whether you will do wholesaling, rental properties, and real estate flipping. The seller will not hand you the property and wait for the money. Just like when purchasing your own personal home, you need to come up with the money that the seller wants to give up the property.

The good news is that there are a lot of different options that you can choose when it comes to financing your real estate investment. Some of the choices that you can work with include the following:

Cold, Hard cash

Cold, hard cash is a method that many people will not use. This is because it takes a long time to come up with a lot of money to purchase a property and to fix it all up before they can rent or sell it. But if you are able to do this, it means that you will not have to worry about paying off a mortgage or dealing with any of the interest or principle that comes with this.

You will be in charge of all of the money that you would need to purchase that property. This method helps you to reduce any debts that you owe on the property, but you will most likely only purchase one property at a time. There is no leverage here, so if the property is worth $100,000, you have to work with that much money upfront for the seller.

The benefit for this one is that you can get the process done faster. You don't have to wait for the bank to finish up with their work before you get the loan. The seller may be willing and able to move faster if they see that they are getting cash without any strings attached.

Again, the negative is that you are tying up all of your money into one property. If it fails, that means that you will lose all of the money that you have invested. If you had used a conventional loan, you could technically get five buildings of $100,000 (You pay 20 percent, which would mean $20,000 each for five properties.) for the same amount of money as using cash for just one property.

Owner Financing

Another option is owner financing. This one is a little harder to get because you have to find a seller who is willing and able to do it. Most sellers want just get done with the house and move on rather than receiving payments for the next few years. Depending on the location and how much trouble the sellers had or think they will have to sell the property, you may be able to find this.

The idea is that the seller will finance the property for you. You will pay them an agreed-upon payment each month that includes interest and more. Then this is a ballooning payment. That means that over time you will have to pay it off faster and faster. Usually, these last for five years. If you are not able to pay it off in five years, then the house goes back to the seller, and they get to enjoy all of the renovations that you did on the property.

As you can see, there is some sort of risk that comes with this. You have to get another loan or do other things to pay off the seller within a few years. Most sellers don't like the idea of not being able to sell the property and earn the big profit right from the beginning. But if you are running into issues with some of the other financing options, this may be the right one for you.

Portfolio Lenders

Next on the list is a portfolio lender. This will be some kind of bank or another kind of institution that will originate the mortgage loan and will hold onto a portfolio of these loans rather than selling them to another, bigger bank. This kind of lender will generate some fees from originating these mortgages, and they will work to make some profits from the net interest rate spread or the difference between the interest-earning assets and the interest paid on deposits in their mortgage portfolio.

Traditionally, most of the mortgage lenders that you will work with will avoid some of the risks that come with actually holding onto the mortgage. They will earn some profits from those origination fees, and then they sell the actual mortgage off to another financial institution.

Of course, there will be some benefits and some negatives that come with both of these options. Companies that profit from starting these mortgages and then handing them off will experience a lot less risk, and they will still earn a good and consistent stream of income in the process. But the portfolio lender will increase their risks in the hopes of making more in profits.

There are a number of benefits that come with using this kind of plan. Some of the benefits that you may notice when you approach one of these portfolio lenders to help you out include the following:

1. Loan approvals: You may find that it is easier to get the loan with one of these lenders compared to a regular bank. This is because the portfolio lender, while still following

some guidelines to avoid risks, will not need to meet the underwriting guidelines that are specified by the buyers in the secondary market.

2. Greater flexibility: Many of these lenders will own banks that are small, privately owned, and local. This means that they will have a bit of flexibility compared to some of the bigger banks.

3. Investor friendly: The mortgages that are offered by these kinds of lenders will be more favorable to investors of the property. For example, they usually don't come with restrictions on how many properties one investor can purchase. They also don't need the property to be in a certain condition before the financing can go on. This can be really helpful for those investors who would like to purchase an older home and fix it up.

Of course, to get all of these benefits, there will be a few limitations with these kinds of loans. First, there will be some prepayment fees. These lenders could charge you a fee if you pay the mortgage off earlier. There are some federal laws that help limit the amount they can charge, and this could end up increasing the overall cost of your loan. Before you originate this kind of loan, see if you are able to negotiate the fees so that you can pay off early or refinance if needed.

In addition, these loans will come with some interest rates that are a little bit higher. This is done to help offset a bit of the risk that the portfolio lender will take on when they service the loan. If the Federal Reserve is increasing the interest rates, it is possible that this kind of lender will increase their variable rates even faster.

Conventional Mortgage

The next option on the list is a conventional mortgage. This would be the same kind of mortgage that you would take out if you were purchasing a home for your own personal use. You can choose between a 15- to 30-year loan, and there are also options for variable and fixed interest rates as well. There are also a few options when it comes to a conventional mortgage that you can work with so talking to your bank will help you pick out the right one for you.

A conventional mortgage is sometimes hard to get, especially with these investment properties, but they often give you the best rates and will reduce your risks. Your job is to fill out the application, provide the necessary information to help the bank make a decision, and ensure that you can pay for your current debts and the new mortgage. You cannot potential income from house flipping or from rental money when figuring out the income, so you have to be careful and get your finances in order for this one.

Having a good credit score, making sure that your debt to income ratio is as low as possible, and working with your banker are important. These loans take some time to get and will often require the building you want to purchase to be in decent shape. But once you get them, they are easier to work with, will have the lowest interest rate out of the other options, and will even allow you to pay them down earlier if you would like.

Hard Money

Hard money is the term that describes a stream of funding that originates from a government agency or some other similar organization. The flow of these funds represents an ongoing and scheduled series of payments rather than receiving all of the money at once. Some examples would be receiving subsidies on daycare or an annual scholarship to college.

Hard money can be the preferred form of funding by the government and a lot of other organizations because it will provide a predictable stream of funds in that process. There are a lot of different ways that you can work with this option, but when it comes to lending, you may find that it is used in a way that is a bit different than the other terms above.

For example, when we are talking about a hard money loan, we are talking about one that has been backed by the value of some kind of asset. This could be a car or a home. The cost of that asset is the collateral for the loan. This ensures that if the investor doesn't pay the money back, then the lender, usually a bank, can take over the asset and sell it to recover some of their money.

You will find that a hard money loan will come with a higher interest rate than what the borrower may get with a traditional mortgage lender or some other kind of financing channel that they may try to use. Private investors and individuals will use this kind of hard money loan as lenders of last resort. If nothing else will work or they are in a crunch on time or finances, then this is the method that they will use. If you can find another method that will work better, then it is best to go with that.

Private Money

A private money lender is a company or an individual—not one tied to a bank—that will be secured by a note and a deed of trust for the purpose of funding a transaction in the real estate market. These lenders will have a bit more of a base in relationships than hard money lenders, which allows you an option to show your case and work with the lender to get things done rather than being all on your own.

One mistake that a lot of new investors in real estate make is that they will spend way too much time learning about how to find and type up new deals but they will spend enough time learning how to raise the capital they need from some private money lenders. This is just as important. You may find the best deal in the world, but if you cannot get the right capital to make it happen, then it will never happen.

While you can work with friends and family you know to help with this kind of lending, it is usually not a good idea. It is always a better idea to work with other investors, ones you are not familiar with and your relationship is not at stake. If you do work with a family member or a friend, make sure that you write it all up and have a contract between the two of you to ensure that you are both on the same page.

A better option is to work with the third party circle. This will be investors who are mostly removed from your network. You have no personal connection with these individuals. This circle will have a lot more capital than what you will find with the other groups, but because they don't know you and are probably bothered by a lot of other investors on a regular basis, it is possible that this group will be the hardest to get money from.

This brings up the question of how you will find these investors if you don't know them from the start. First, you can look at some of the contact sites for investors. BiggerPockets, LendingClub, Go Big Network and more can all help. This ensures that you can post about your opportunity to invest, and then you can actively contact other investors. However, make sure that you keep your contact professional and that it fits in with the SEC for both state and federal levels to keep yourself safe

Another creative approach that you can use is the investor direct mail list. This is when you will work with a list broker to ascertain if there is already a list of potential investors who will meet your criteria before you work with them.

203K Loans

The next option is the 203K loan. This is not a type of retirement loan even though it may seem that way at first. Instead, it is a type of loan that you can get that helps you wrap up some or all of the costs that you will need to renovate the property into one loan with one closing cost. The amount that you end up borrowing with this will include the price of the property and the estimated amount for repairs, including what you would pay for materials and labor.

The down payment that you would do on this kind of loan will depend on the full amount that the bank will give you for everything. You will notice that the monthly payments will come in a bit higher, but this is because you are technically combining two different loans into one.

Now, this one will be a bit harder to receive because it is for a higher amount. You need to take a look at the standards of your lender to help you figure out whether or not you qualify. Usually, you need a credit score of 640 or higher, and your debt to income ratio, including the amount you owe with the new debt, needs to be less than 43 percent. The full amount that you get for the loan also needs to be no higher than the maximum limit for an FHA loan in your area.

Just like with any of the other FHA loans that you may apply for, you will need to fill out an application and show complete documentation of your income and any assets along with your credit profile. Of course, since you are getting money to renovate a new property, you will also need to include a cost estimate. The appraiser for the bank will estimate the value of the home and how it is doing in the current state and then come up with an estimate of how much the home will be worth based on the costs of the renovation.

If you would like to combine some of the renovations of your new property with the mortgage, then this is one of the options that you need to consider. It is easy to work with, and you will not have to find two separate loans in the process although it is a bit harder to get since your mortgage will be higher and you have to deal with higher payments at the same time.

FHA Loans

When we talk about an FHA loan, we look at a mortgage that has been insured by the Federal Housing Administration. These will be popular for first time home buyers because they allow for low down payments, usually at 3.5 percent, and the credit score of the borrower can be lower than 600 in some cases. However, when using this kind of loan, you will need to pay an insurance premium on the mortgage to help protect the lender if you default on the loan.

This kind of loan program was created as a response to all of the defaults and foreclosures that happened in the 1930s to help mortgage lenders have the right amount of insurance and to ensure that the housing market would keep going up. The lenders provided more affordable and accessible loans even to those who didn't have a lot of money saved up or less than perfect credit.

Essentially, these loans will be made with insurance from the federal government. This makes the banks and other lenders more likely to give out this kind of loan because they know they can get the money back even if there are some problems that show up later with the borrower. You do need to meet a few requirements, such as being a lawful citizen in this country, have a good work history, and more, but it is a great way to get into the housing market and start your investment without having to come up with the full 20 percent down.

Partnerships

If you know of someone else or maybe a few people who would be willing to do the real estate endeavor together, this may be a great way to get into the market without having quite as much money to get things started.

With this method, you and one or more other people will get the funding that you need. Maybe all of you can pool together the money to purchase a property, using your own savings and capital along the way. Or maybe you will work together to get the mortgage or another loan that is needed to get this started.

Banks may look more favorably at two or more people purchasing a property together rather than just one person who is doing all of it on their own. This means that two people can be held liable for the property and they will more likely pay the money back. This represents less risk to the bank. If you can get three or four people together to do this, it is an even better way to get started.

Since everyone took out a loan or put up their own capital to purchase the property, when the income starts to come in, either monthly from the rental unit or all at once from flipping a house, that profit will be divided up amongst all of you. If one person gives more than the others, make sure to divide it up based on how much each person contributed. (This should be something discussed ahead of time and written into the contract that you all share.)

Home Equity Loans

If you already own a property of your own, working with a home equity loan can be a great option for you. These kinds of loans can allow the investor to borrow against the value of your home over the amount of any mortgages of the property. So, if your home is worth $150,000 and you owe a mortgage of $135,000, then your equity in the property would be $15,000.

Depending on how long you have owned the home, how much you have paid off, the original down payment, and how the housing market is doing in your area, it is possible to take out a large amount of money based on the equity of your home. Often it is easier to qualify for one of these types of loans because the house becomes the security for you.

You have to think about this as a second type of mortgage. Your first mortgage will be the one that you used to purchase your property. You can then use the additional loans to purchase against the home, but you have to make sure that you are doing this in a smart manner and that you have built up enough equity. Of course, there will be some risk that comes with this, so it should not be the first option.

There are two options that you can use when it comes to a home equity loan. The first one is to take a big lump sum of cash right up front and then repay that loan over time with some fixed monthly payments. You will have a set interest rate when you borrow, and you will see the rate stay the same until the loan is paid off. Each monthly payment will reduce the balance of the loan and will cover some of the interest.

It is also possible to work with a home equity line of credit. This is like a credit card that will tell you the maximum amount that you can use and then you just take the amount that you need from that. This option will allow you to borrow more than one time, if it is needed, once you are approved. You will start by making some smaller payments in the beginning, but then you will need to balloon those payments to eliminate the loan.

The repayment terms that you get will depend on the type of loan that you get. You will need to make a fixed monthly payment for the first type, and these usually last for 10 years. You will have to talk with your lender to figure out how long you get to pay back the loan. It is always best to pay it back faster than slower in case something happens with the property or you need money for something else.

As you can see, this is a great way to get the money that you need to build up your real estate empire. But there are some drawbacks. First off, it is possible that you will lose your home if you cannot stick with the chosen monthly payment schedule. If you cannot repay, the bank may foreclose on your home so that they can regain any missing money.

It is also tempting to use your home as a kind of ATM because these loans will provide you with a ton of cash. But you should be selective with when you plan to use these. It may work fine for real estate but have a plan in place for paying it all back. Otherwise, it is too easy to keep taking and using the money for silly things rather than using it to grow your business, and this can cost you down the line.

Retirement Accounts

If you are running out of options and you have exhausted all of your other choices, one place you may want to look is your retirement account. There are a lot of experts in the field who will tell you not to do this because of the risk. But if you are certain that you have found a good deal that you are not willing to let go and really want to get that market going, then working with your retirement account may be a good option.

The idea is that you use some of the money that has been accumulating in your retirement account and put it towards the down payment or even the full payment of the property you would like to invest in. When you work in this manner, you can take the money out right away and not have to worry about working with a bank at all.

If you do choose to work with this method, consider only taking out the interest that you have earned on the account, not the principal. This allows the money that you have put in to continue growing and sets a limit for how much you have taken out.

You have to consider how much this could potentially hurt you in the future. If you take out an early withdrawal, which is any time you take money out of a traditional IRA before you reach the age of 59½, then you will have taxes and fees on the money. You need to talk with your financial advisor to figure out if the amount that you want to take out is worth the time and the money that you will need to pay in fees.

When you take money out of a retirement account, it is also taking money away from what you can earn for your retirement. This is money that could be accumulating in your account. If you take it out, that is gone. Deciding if this is a good risk will be a personal opinion, but it is still something to consider.

Commercial Loans

Finally, we need to look at something known as a commercial loan. This is a debt-based funding arrangement that occurs between one financial institution and a business. It is often used as a way to fund big capital expenditures and to cover some of the operational costs that the company may struggle to pay for on its own.

Keep in mind that it can be hard for smaller businesses to d0 this. There are a lot of hurdles in the form of regulations and upfront costs, and this can make it harder to do.

These commercial loans can be given to a lot of entities in businesses. Often, they will be used as a way to assist with a lot of the short-term funding that is needed or for some of the operational costs to purchase things, like equipment to keep the business going. In some cases, it is possible that this kind of loan will be extended to help a particular business meet some of its basic operational needs, such as funding payroll or purchasing supplies.

For the business to get this kind of a loan, it needs to post some collateral. It may use equipment, the plant, or the property. It can be anything of value that the bank can take away from the borrower if the person can't pay the loan. Sometimes, depending on the kind of business that is in question, the cash flows generated from future accounts receivable will be enough to use as collateral.

As you can see, there are many different options when it comes to getting the funding that you need to start in the real estate world.

There are a lot of options that come with it, and choosing the one that you like depends on the rates that you want, your credit score, what you want to do with the property, and more. Make sure to do your research ahead of time to ensure that you know the different options and that you can pick the one that will work the best for you.

CHAPTER 7:

Planning Your Exit Strategy

At some point in this game, you will want to exit the market and sell the property that you have. If you are flipping homes, you will use your exit strategy early on and get rid of the properties you purchase on a regular basis to make money. Even if you are working with a rental property, there may come a time when you no longer want one property or another, and you would rather sell it.

It is important for you to go through and come up with an exit strategy that will work the best for your needs. Each investor will handle things a bit differently, and that will vary depending on the kind of investment strategy you went with in the first place. Planning your exit strategy can be so important to ensure that you can get as much out of this process as possible for all of your hard work. Some of the things that you can consider when it comes to planning your exit strategy include the following:

Traditional Selling with an Agent

Many times, especially when you are first getting started with your real estate empire, you may want to work with a realtor. This can provide you with many advantages and can ensure that you will not have to spend too much of your time and energy doing all of the work on your own.

There are a number of benefits that you can get when you work with a real estate agent. These individuals can post on their own websites and on the MLS to make sure that your property gets the maximum amount of exposure in a short amount of time. You will find that these agents also have a list (from their own efforts of networking) of potential buyers who may be interested in your property. They can call these people and see if they're interested in the property.

Most of the time, you can sell the property much faster if you work with an agent. They are specialists when it comes to the real estate market, and they know how to get the property sold faster than you. Working with a good agent from the buying process all the way to the selling process is a great idea because it ensures that you are making the right improvements and renovations to the property without the risk of wasting time or money.

After some time, when you gain your own network of potential buyers and sellers and get better at running the empire you are creating, you may decide to work without an agent, and you may want to do the selling on your own. But you will find that it is a lot more work for you to do it on your own rather than trusting an agent to do it for you.

One of the biggest reasons that an investor, or any other kind of seller for that matter, will not choose to work with a real estate agent is to save money. When you sell a property and use an agent, you will pay them commission, usually around five to six percent of the sale price on the property. This will cut into some of your potential profits if you are working with an agent. You have to determine if you can afford this amount out of your profits and figure out if it is a good idea for you.

Selling for Sale by Owner (FSBO)

If you choose to sell your home or property without working with an agent, then you would sell with a for sale by owner or FSBO. If the market is going pretty fast and inventory is going pretty quick, then this may be the best option for you.

The issue that most FSBO will find is that it is hard to find buyers. Plus, you have to worry about contract acceptance and closing along the way as well. Not every seller will be good for working with this kind of process. But a good market will make this easier. The worst thing that will happen here is that you will sell your home for too little and you will not earn as much as you should.

You could also run into some complications depending on how the home inspection goes.

Not all sellers, especially ones who are brand new to the process, will be successful with this option. For example, according to the National Association of Realtors, it is believed that the majority of FSBO properties end up getting listed with a realtor after some time. The reason for this in most cases is that most home buyers you find will use an agent to represent them. Another reason is that the owners of these properties will not have the expertise to make sure that they are doing the work right.

There are a lot of things that you need to deal with when it comes to selling on your own. You have to figure out a good market price for the property. Since you are an investor who purchased this property, you should already have a good idea of how much you can sell the property. Consider if this is high enough and with a bit more research if it is still at a good price.

Then you need to spend some time preparing the property. If you are living in the property, you need to make sure that you are getting all of your things cleaned up and looking nice each time that someone wants to look at the property. If you are not living in the property, then this will not be a good deal because the property should stay nice with no one living there.

You need to prepare the property as much as possible. You need to walk into the property and look at it from the viewpoint of a stranger. Ask a friend for help, someone who isn't as attached to all of the hard work that was done inside as you may be. You may even consider working with staging. If you don't live in the property, adding in some furniture to show the potential buyer how the property can look can make a difference. Make it look like someone is living there, if possible, rather than an empty building that you want to sell.

Since you are saving some money by not having an agent help you to sell the property, you should consider doing a bit of marketing to make this easier. You need to market the property as much as possible to find the right buyer. You can first market in a newspaper, online with social media, and other listing sites. Take good pictures of the property and showcase the property and all that it has to offer.

Get creative. A real estate agent has a lot of different networking abilities, and they know how to put their resources to good work. Since you are new to all of this, you may not have built this all up yet. This means that you need to get a bit creative and find the buyers in locations where you may not have thought of. Don't be afraid to think outside the box and try something new.

One thing that you may consider spending money on is a real estate attorney. Having them create the forms that you need, both for buying and selling a property, will make things easier. They can make a template for you to use to legally protect you as the buyer and as the seller as well as the other party in both cases. If you get these templates prepared ahead of time, you can use them for the majority of the purchases and sales that you do.

The 1031 Exchange

Another option that you may want to look at is the 1031 exchange. This is a transaction when a taxpayer can exchange one investment property for another by deferring the consequences of a tax of a sale. This is authorized by the IRS Code as long as it is used in the proper manner.

There are a few rules that you will have to follow to work with this kind of exchange. First, you need to worry about timelines. The investor needs to follow the 45/180-day guideline for the exchange. Once they relinquish the property, the seller will have 45 days to find a property that is of equal or greater value. Once they find it, they have no more than 180 days from the day they sold their property to finish acquiring the new property.

Another requirement is that the investor needs to find what is known as like-kind property. This means that it must be other qualifying forms of real estate. So, you could sell a duplex and then purchase a new commercial property. Or you could sell a piece of land and then move on to an apartment building. The goal is that the property needs to be like-kind.

The exchange property, or the one that you are switching to, needs to be held for investment. These both need to be investments that are used for the purpose of your business. This means that you cannot use this to sell off your primary residence and then purchase an investment property. It can't go the other way around either. You cannot sell an investment property and get a personal property either.

During this kind of exchange, there needs to be an equal or greater debt and equity that is present. This means that if you sell a property for $1 million and $500,000 was equity and $500,000 was debt, then you will need to purchase property worth $1 million or more. You also need to use all of your equity and replace all of the debt to defer all of the capital gain taxes.

There are some risks with working with this kind of exchange in your own life. It will not always work out the way that you like. If your numbers will not work the way that you thought and your calculations are off, you will run into some issues with paying the capital gains tax. It is important to plan this and to know what you are doing before you work with this option over one of the others.

Selling with Seller Financing

We talked a bit earlier about how you can ask the seller to finance the property so that you can purchase it. Now it is time to consider whether you would like to do some seller financing to get rid of a property that you own and to make a good income in the process. It is not very often that you will find sellers who want to work with the idea of seller financing. It can be a scary thing to work with and is often misunderstood. But depending on your goals and how many buyers you attract, it may be an option that you will want to consider.

This is a great alternative to working with a traditional financing tool, and it can be useful in locations or at times when getting a mortgage can be hard. This allows the seller to tap into a new population of buyers who cannot get a home in any other manner, and it helps the buyers find a new form of credit to purchase the home. Because the seller is the one financing the sale, they may be able to get a higher sales price than with other options along the way.

When you work with a seller-financed sale, a bank will not be directly involved because the seller and the buyer will make all of the arrangements on their own. They will draw up a promissory note that sets out the schedule of payments from the buyer to the seller, the interest rate, and the consequences if the buyer does not meet these obligations. There will not be any principal that is switched over from the buyer to the seller—just an agreement to repay the sum over time.

There are a few benefits to this. There are only two players involved, which means that it will be a cheaper and faster option compared to using the traditional manner. The closing costs and origination fees will also be a lot lower than some of the other methods.

If you are the seller working in this kind of situation, there are a few things that you can keep in mind. First, you will not need to finance the sale for long. As the seller, you get the option of selling this promissory note to a lender or investor, and then the buyer will send the payments there. This means that you do not need to have the cash here or become the lender. However, if you do this, remember that it is possible that you will accept less than the full value of that note to get it sold. This will reduce the return that you can get for this property, but if you want out, it is something to consider.

You can also consider making the seller financing part something that you add into your pitch to sell the property. Since this is a rare thing that is not seen that much, promote that you are offering it. When a potential buyer sees this, you can talk to them about the financing details a bit more if you would like. This may get a few more people to look at your listing and consider making an offer.

Sometimes these kinds of deals will pose a bit of complication when it is time to do your taxes. Talking about how this can affect you with a tax expert or a financial planner will be the key that you need to ensure that you can keep yourself safe when it is time to sell the property that you want.

At some point, you may be ready to sell the property that you are investing in. Whether you are a landlord and looking to let go of the property after making some money on it for some time or you are flipping a home and want it gone quickly, knowing your plan and sticking with it will make a big difference in how much you make. Follow some of the tips in this guidebook, and you can see success when it is time to exit the property.

CHAPTER 8:

Making It Passive

The ultimate goal when you get started in the real estate market is to find a way to turn it into a passive income source. You will find that the real estate market will be one of the best ways to earn a passive income the way that you want. With the help of a few properties under your belt and a good property manager, you can earn any income that you want.

Being your own boss, picking out a good property manager, learning how to work smarter rather than harder, and working on the different steps that you can take to turn this into a passive income is so important when you get into the real estate market. In fact, when you first get into this kind of market, that should be the overall goal that you work towards. When you get to this chapter, you should be ready to make it into the ultimate passive income source.

Be the Boss

The neat thing about growing your own real estate empire is that you are the one who gets to be the boss. You are growing your own business, and you get to be the one who sets your own hours, decide which properties you want to work with, and even choose which tenants you would like to work with in your properties as well.

That is one of the best things that you will find when it comes to working with real estate is that it allows you to be the boss and control your own hours and your own income. If you would like to earn more income, you can choose to purchase another property and work from there, or if the market allows for it, you can raise the rent on a few of the properties that you already have and earn more from those.

In the beginning, you are the one who has to spend a lot of your time and energy on the properties. You won't make a lot in the beginning, and you want to make sure that you are reinvesting it all and getting the results that you want. You have to pick out the property and do all of the research that comes with it. You have to pick out the tenants, choose the rental price, maintain the building, collect the rent, and more, and you will probably continue doing this for the first few properties or more that you own.

But if you are creating your own business and empire with this, you will get the benefit of becoming the boss. When you have a good income and own several properties that are earning a good amount of money from it at the same time, it may be time to turn the work over to someone else to help you out.

This is the ultimate goal of working in real estate, and it is one of the main reasons that a lot of investors will choose to work with real estate in the first place rather than one of the other investment options. You can truly turn this into a passive income, and the best way to do this is to hire a good property manager to make it happen. The property manager will do everything for you, and you can be the boss during the whole process.

Your property manager can take over all of the work that you do with these rental properties. They are often more efficient at it because they are more of a manager than one landlord, and they have a good system to make it happen. You could do the work on your own, but if you would like to gain some financial freedom with this endeavor and do not want to spend a lot of time doing all of this, you will find that a property manager is the best option for you.

A property manager can save you a lot of time and effort. They will help you find the tenants that your properties need and will ensure the proper background checks are done ahead of time. They will collect the rent, get all of the routine checks done, maintain the properties, and so much more. Anything that needs to be done with the properties, whether it is the structure itself or with the tenants, the property manager can do it for you.

Now, you may need to be careful with choosing the right property manager that you decide to hire. You want to make sure that you get someone who knows what they are doing, who has experience in the field and who has some good customer service experience. Research some of the different property managers who are available in your area and do an interview with them to figure out who you will work with for the long term.

You also want to take a look at the fee structure of the property managers. Most of them will be pretty similar, but you may find that one has better fees than others. Remember that they will usually ask for a percentage of the total rent that you get from any properties that they manage. If you are working with a single-family home or a small multi-family home, it is likely they will take about 10 percent of the rent. If you ask them to work with a bigger apartment building, they may take a smaller percentage since the rent is more overall.

Working Hard vs. Working Smart

The next thing that we need to take a look at is the difference between working hard and working smart. This is an area that a lot of beginners will struggle with. They think that they have to work at breakneck speeds all the time. But this is miserable, and it is not necessary when it comes to starting your own real estate business. There will be a level of sweat and hard work that goes into starting this. But over time, as you learn the ropes and gain more and more properties, you will learn the difference between working hard and working smart.

Your goal is to work smart. You may still need to work hard, but you will not have to work as hard as some others when you get your whole process under control and have some organization. One way that you can do this, for example, is to have a property manager. This person will handle a lot of the different parts of the investment for you. You can monitor them and make sure they are on your own system, and then you can still earn your money without having to do as much work.

Even without a property manager, you can work smart instead of harder. If you can create a good screening system for tenants, have a checklist to help you pick out which properties you will work with, and are organized, you will find that it is easier than ever to earn the money that you want without having to work yourself to death.

Filling Spaces – Always Keeping your Real Estate Filled

One of the most important and the most challenging things that you will need to do as a landlord is make sure that your properties stay filled. It doesn't matter how many you own or how big you are growing your business or empire, you will find that if there are no tenants in them, you will end up losing money. Even if the mortgage is paid off, you will find that you still need to pay for things like maintenance, taxes, and insurance, so you want to make sure that you have a good plan in place to get good tenants who will stay.

First, you need to make sure that your system is smart and organized when it comes to picking out your tenants. A good tenant will make your job easier, and you will feel like you are not actually doing any work. A bad tenant will make it so that you need to worry about issues like not getting rent, having to deal with the time and costs of evictions, and more.

Finding a good tenant does take some time. In the long run, even though it can be frustrating, you may find that it is better to have the apartment stay empty for a bit longer rather than choose a bad tenant. As a landlord, remember that the tenant will be a big determinant in how well the investment goes, so taking your time and learning about each applicant can make a difference.

For example, you need to do background checks on each potential tenant. Find out if they have ever had an eviction in the past. If they have, it is likely that they will cause you some problems again so you probably don't want to work with them. You should also check their income to make sure that they have a steady work history and that they can afford the rent.

When you have a tenant who you would like to move into the property, make sure that they sign a lease. This document will protect you and the tenant, so it is a good thing for both parties. It will outline the rules and responsibilities and the expectations of both of you so that no one is confused about what they can expect during this time. If you have a potential tenant who is not willing to sign the lease, then it is best to walk away and work with someone else.

The best thing that you can do when working on your real estate empire is to make sure that you keep up a constant list of people who may be potential renters down the line. This can make it a lot faster when it is time to pull someone in when a building becomes empty. In an ideal world, you would find one tenant who would stay in the building or the property forever. But that is not reality. People decide to move to a bigger place or a new part of town, get a job in another state, decide to purchase a home, or something similar.

If you network and learn more about a lot of different people in the area and maybe even hold onto some of the names of those who have applied with you in the past (with their knowledge and permission, of course), then it may be much easier for you to find someone who can move in quickly after the former tenant moves out.

This is the number one thing that you will learn about being a landlord. The longer the property is without a tenant, the more it will cost you. If you can keep tenants in the property for a longer period of time and fill up any vacancies with other good tenants quickly as tenants leave, you will be more likely to make a lot of money in the process.

The overall goal that you need to work towards is growing your empire. And the good news is that if you work hard in the beginning and you are willing to put in the time and effort, then you will find that things will get a lot easier over time. You need to be dedicated, and you need to always be a part of the investment. If you can do this, you will see some amazing results with how quickly your business can grow.

Conclusion

Thank for making it through to the end of *Real Estate Investing Crash Course*. Let's hope it was informative and provided you with all of the tools you need to achieve your goals whatever they may be.

The next step is to start planning the strategy that you would like to use when it is time to work in the real estate market. There are so many different opportunities that you can work in this market and so many chances to make money. But picking out the one that you would like to do the most will be so critical to your overall success. This guidebook will show you how to get started for all of the success that you could ever wish for.

This guidebook took some time to talk about all of the different things that you need to know about the real estate market. Whether you have been investing for some time or you are brand new to the whole arena, you will find that this guidebook is the tool that you need to see the best results in no time.

When you are ready to learn how to grow your own real estate empire from the very beginning all the way through until you can earn a full-time passive income, make sure to check out this guidebook to help you get started today!

Finally, if you found this book useful in any way, a review is always appreciated!

www.ingramcontent.com/pod-product-compliance
Lightning Source LLC
Chambersburg PA
CBHW020554220526
45463CB00006B/2304